MW01708491

THE eyespy BOOK OF NIGHT CREATURES

Chris Cheng

Illustrated by Michael Davis

ASHTON SCHOLASTIC

SYDNEY AUCKLAND NEW YORK TORONTO LONDON

CONTENTS

Hi, kids!

Welcome to the fascinating world of nocturnal animals—those animals which are more active at night-time than daytime. You'll meet bilbies, possums, pythons, hopping mice, quolls, bats, owls, cuscuses and many other amazing creatures.

To celebrate we're going to have a party—a nocturnal party. Ask your friends to come masked and dressed as their favourite nocturnal animals.

On the activity pages following each animal you will find games to play, food to cook, stencils for animal masks, and decorations to make—all with a nocturnal flavour.

So come along and join in the fun.

Chris

BILBY

The bilby, also known as the rabbit-eared bandicoot because of its long ears, is a small nocturnal marsupial. It has soft blue-grey fur and a long snout. To make up for its poor eyesight, the bilby has a keen sense of smell and acute hearing.

The bilby eats insects, fruits, and seeds which it licks up with its long thin tongue. It has powerful front legs with strong claws which it uses to dig for food around termite mounds and spinifex tussocks, and for burrowing. The bilby digs the ground with its front legs and uses its back legs to kick the soil away. It is the only member of the bandicoot family to make a permanent burrow.

The female bilby has a backwardly opening pouch. Usually only two young are born in a litter. The young bilbies leave the pouch when they are about ten weeks old and then stay in the burrow until they are old enough to fend for themselves.

The bilby is scattered throughout the deserts of central Australia and is now an endangered species.

BILBY'S BASH

Invite your friends over for a night of nocturnal fun and games. But first you should make and send out your invitations.

What you need:
A4 paper or card
felt-tip pens
scissors

What to do:
Trace the outline of the bilby on page 7 onto card. Cut out the outline, draw in the features, as shown, and colour it a light blue-grey. Write the party details on the back. It should read something like this:

> Come and join in the fun at:
> *Bilby's Bash*
> on ______________________
> at ______________________
> Come masked as your favourite night animal.
> RSVP

BILBY MASK

Using the grid on page 7, transfer the outline of the bilby's head onto a strong piece of card. Cut out the shape and attach a string through the holes on the side of the head. The mask will stay in position as long as you make sure the string goes above your ears. Cut out holes where the eyes are marked.

A bilby has long, silky blue-grey fur so see if you can match up your mask with blue-grey T-shirt and track-suit pants. A long tail, made out of an old stocking stuffed with tissue paper and painted white on the toe (the tip), can be pinned on to your track suit pants and will make you look the bilby part.

Your friends can copy the mask stencils for the other animals in this book and match them up with appropriately coloured T-shirts and track-suit pants for their nocturnal animal costumes.

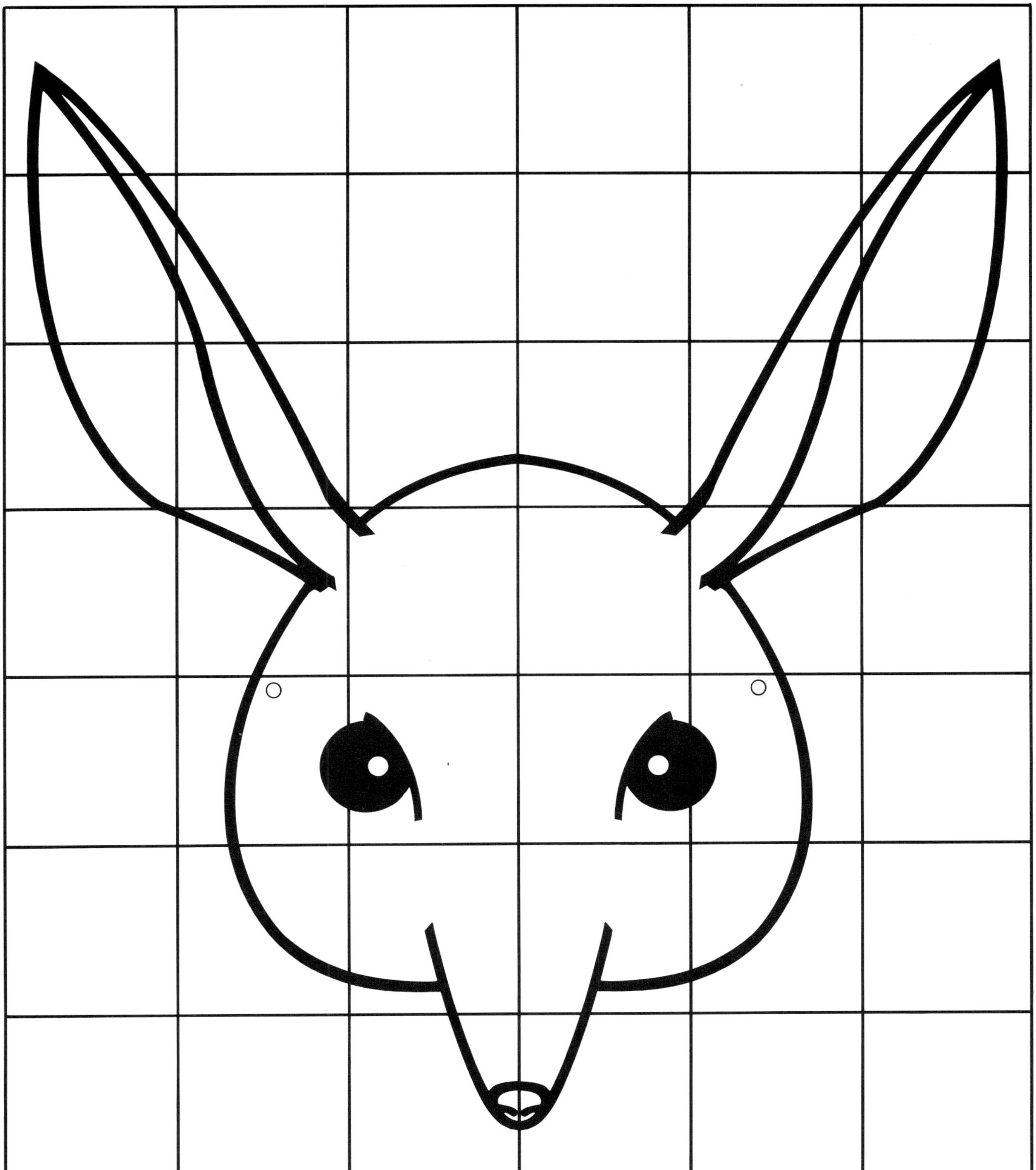

BRUSH-TAILED PHASCOGALE

This small marsupial with its big dishlike eyes, tall ears, naked nose and long large whiskers is well suited to nocturnal life. At night it hunts for spiders, centipedes and small birds to eat.

The phascogale makes its nest of shredded bark and leaves in hollow trees.

Instead of a pouch, the female phascogale has folds of soft skin surrounding her eight nipples. More than eight young are born but only those strong enough to attach themselves to a nipple survive. The young come off the nipples after forty days and then stay in the nest until they emerge five months later.

The brush-tailed phascogale lives in forest and open woodlands of southern and northern Australia.

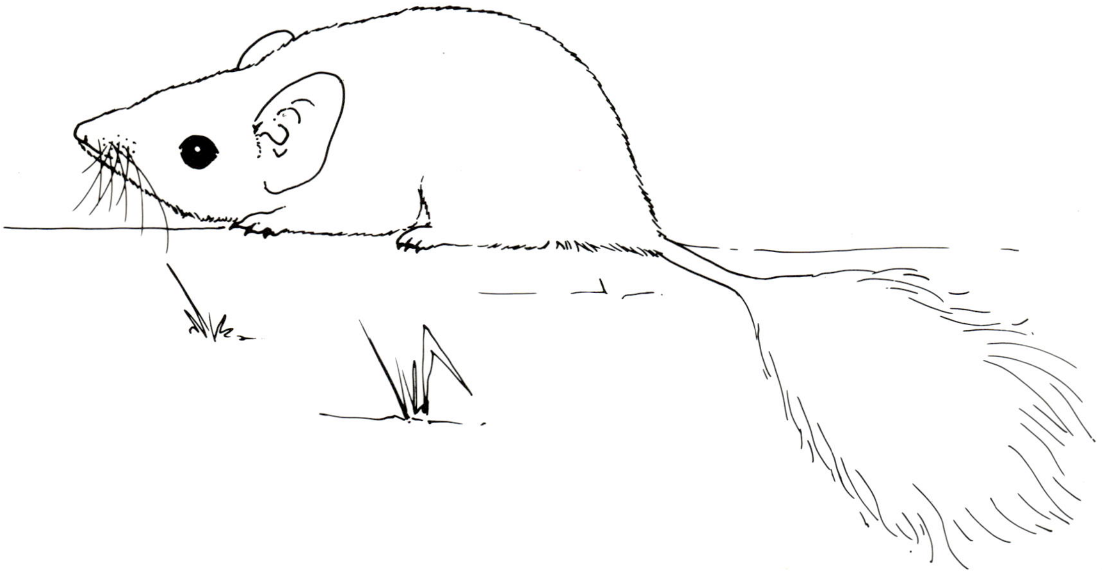

THE BUSH AT NIGHT

Brush-tailed phascogales live in hollows in trees and logs. You can transform your garage, with your parents' permission, into the world of the bush at night. A world the phascogale would feel at home in.

Trees, branches and logs

What you need:

as many cardboard cartons as you can find
felt-tip pens
glue
scissors
stapler
friendly, obedient adult

What to do:

Flatten the cardboard cartons carefully. Draw the outlines of tree trunks, logs and branches of all sizes on the cardboard. Ask the adult to help you cut out the outlines. Staple or glue together the pieces of cardboard to make tall trees and long logs. Draw in knots and black holes on the tree trunks, as shown, using a black felt-tip pen.

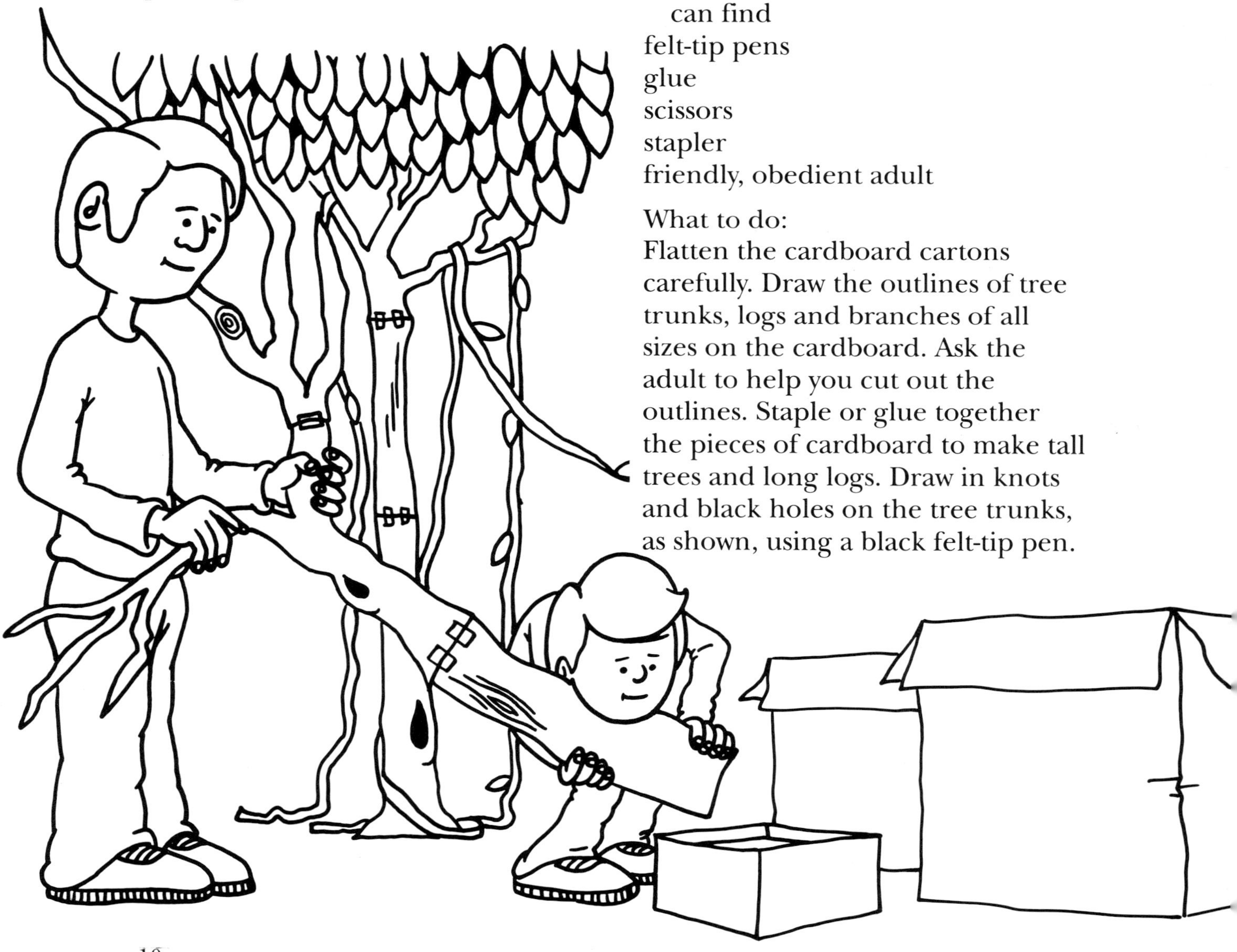

Leaves and vines

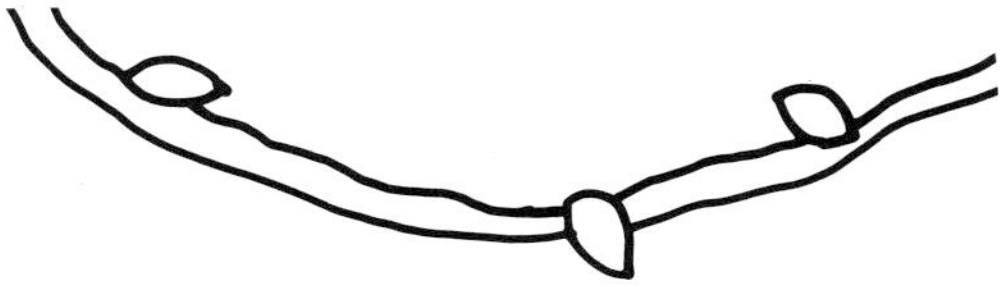

What you need:
green crepe paper
green streamers
brown paper
glue
Blu-tak
felt-tip pens
scissors
friendly, obedient adult

What to do:
Draw and cut out stencils of the leaves shown. Place the stencils on the brown paper and the green crepe paper and cut out leaves. Glue the leaves to the tree trunks and branches.

Stand the trees up against the garage walls, if necessary use Blu-tak to keep them in place.

To create a rainforest atmosphere, you can attach long dangling green and brown streamers from the ceiling.

To give the effect of a true blue night light, ask the adult to help you stick blue Cellophane over the light. Make sure the Cellophane does not touch the bulb, only the shade.

Brush-tailed phascogale mask

Draw a grid on a large piece of card and then copy the outline square by square. Cut around the outline, cut holes for the eyes and mouth and draw in the other features.

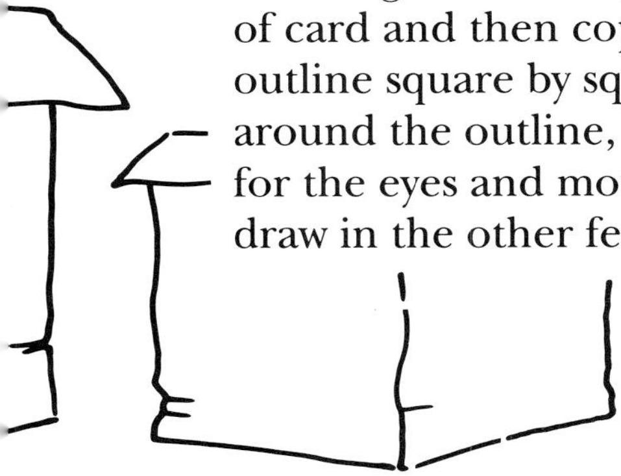

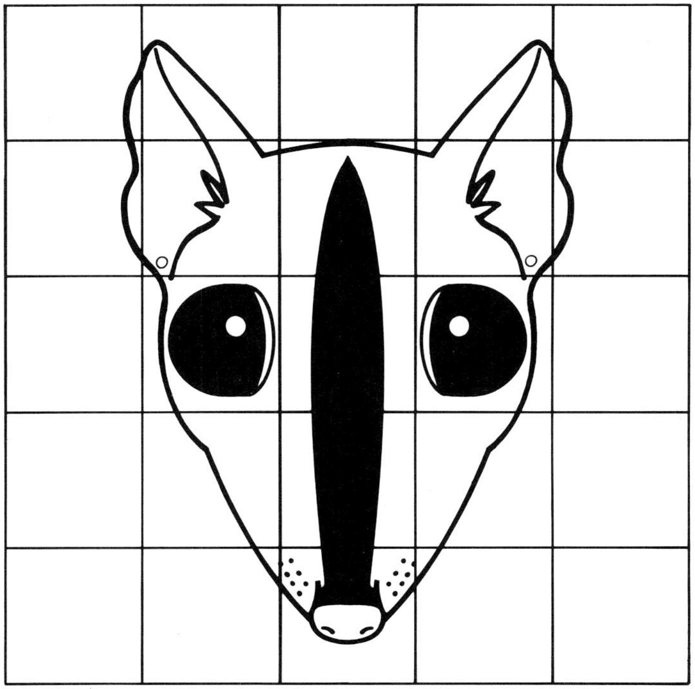

BRUSHTAIL POSSUM

This possum is one of the few native creatures that have adapted very well to living with humans. Not only do these possums like eating the same food as us, such as grapes and cakes, but they also like to live in the roofs of our houses. People who have these possums living nearby often hear them scampering across their roofs at night.

The brushtail possum spends most of the daytime nesting in hollow logs or tree trunks. At night it roams through the bush looking for food. Brushtails sometimes travel on the ground but mostly they move quickly through the trees, using their tails to help them grip branches as they go. In the wild they eat eucalypt leaves, native fruits and buds.

Usually only one possum per litter is born. The young possum spends four to five months in the female's pouch, attached to one of the two teats, and then for one to two months it will ride on its mother's back.

This marsupial is common throughout Australia. Unfortunately it has been introduced into New Zealand where it is now a pest.

POSSUM CUBBY HOUSES

When we tidy up our gardens by trimming trees and lopping off dead branches we may be destroying the nests and shelters of many native animals. Follow these simple instructions and you can create extra homes in your garden for these animals.

What you need:
friendly, helpful adult
plywood
- 2 pieces 20 x 45 cm (front and back)
- 2 pieces 30 x 45 cm (sides)
- 1 piece 20 x 50 cm (top)
- 1 piece 20 x 30 cm (floor)
- 1 piece 14 x 10 cm (front ledge)

glue

What to do:
Ask the hardware shop if they will cut the plywood to size for you. Have the adult cut out a hole, 10 cm in diameter and 5 cm down from the top, in one of the pieces of plywood 20 x 45 cm. This will be the front of the nesting box. After

Brushtail possum mask

Draw a grid on a large piece of card and then copy the outline square by square. Cut around the outline, cut holes for the eyes and mouth and draw in the other features.

the hole is cut, glue the front ledge 8 cm down from the hole.

Glue the remaining pieces of plywood together as shown in diagram 1.

Have the adult help you attach your nesting box to a tree which you know possums visit. Make sure you put some food inside. Possums like to eat soft fruit, like bananas, grapes, pears and apples. You can also put in some native blossoms from grevillea and bottlebrush bushes.

An upturned bucket with a lid also makes a good possum home.

What you need:
plastic bucket
lid
rope
sharp knife
glue
friendly, helpful adult

What do to:
Cut a hole 10 cm in diameter and 10 cm from the base of the bucket, as shown in diagram 2. Punch holes in the lid of the bucket and then glue the lid on firmly. Place the bucket cubby on a branch next to the tree's trunk. Tie it firmly to the trunk with the rope. See diagram 3.

COMMON WOMBAT

This solid, tough burrowing marsupial is closely related to the koala.

The wombat spends the daytime in its burrow and comes out at night to feed, usually on grasses and roots. The wombat's teeth, which have to grind up these tough foods, continue to grow throughout its life.

The wombat's short powerful legs with their flat sturdy claws are well suited to digging. When making a burrow, the wombat uses all four feet to clear away the dirt. If it is attacked the wombat will sometimes scamper head first into the burrow and then use its hard tough rump to block the passage.

The female wombat has a rear opening pouch, so no dirt can get inside while she burrows. The young wombat spends six months in the pouch. Even after it has left the pouch the young wombat will stay with its mother for up to a year before it becomes independent.

The common wombat lives in the forest areas of south-eastern Australia and Tasmania.

BURROW BORROWING

Wombats live in burrows, lots of burrows and they all have different uses. Some burrows are large and some are small. Often they are only the result of a wombat trying to dig a hole to sleep in. Wombats roam between their different burrows each night and sometimes a wombat will use another wombat's burrow.

Who visits your burrow?

Your house is a bit like the wombat's home range. You have lots of rooms that could be burrows. Write down all the 'burrows' that you visit in an afternoon. Count the number of times that you visit each 'burrow'. Now stay in one room and tally the number of 'wombats' which visit that 'burrow'. You may even like to work out which is the most visited 'burrow' in your house.

IN THE DARK

Play a quiz game featuring nocturnal animals with your friends. Write up quiz cards about each animal featured in this book. Make the questions simple and clear. For example.

Question: which nocturnal animal has long rabbit-like ears?

Answer: the bilby.

You can play the game with three of your friends as contestants trying to answer the questions, or you can use the cards as the basis for a board game like Trivial Pursuit.

Common wombat mask

Draw a grid on a large piece of card and then copy the outline square by square. Cut around the outline, cut holes for the eyes and mouth and draw in the other features.

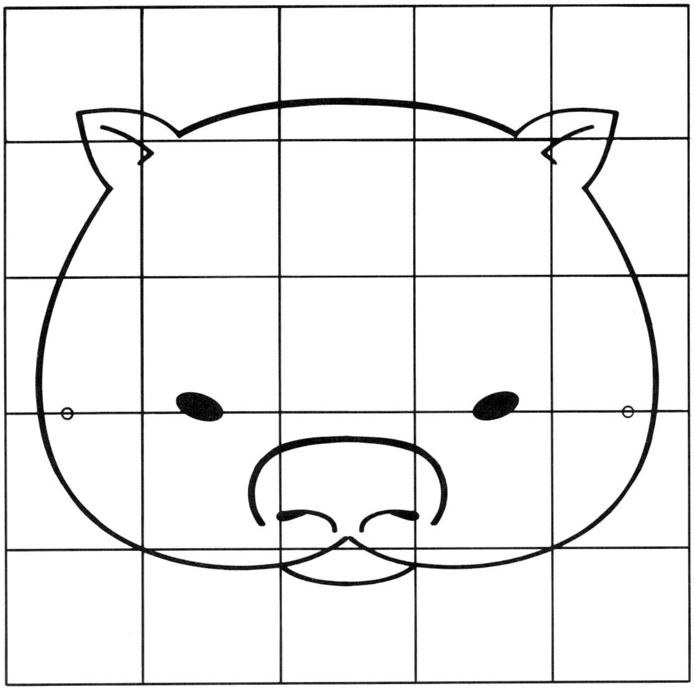

DIAMOND PYTHON

The diamond python, like all pythons, is non-venomous. To kill its prey this snake grabs hold of an animal with its teeth and then coils its body around the animal, gradually squeezing tighter and tighter until it suffocates. Like most snakes, pythons can dislocate their jaws so that they can swallow prey much bigger than themselves. Unlike humans they don't eat every day. In fact, diamond pythons may go all winter without eating at all.

This snake spends much of its time in trees, but it may also live in burrows made by other animals.

When the diamond python has laid a clutch of eggs it will coil its body around them to keep them warm and safe. Once hatched the young python has to fend for itself. An adult diamond python may be up to four metres long.

The diamond python is found in most parts of Australia except the arid centre, southern Victoria and Tasmania.

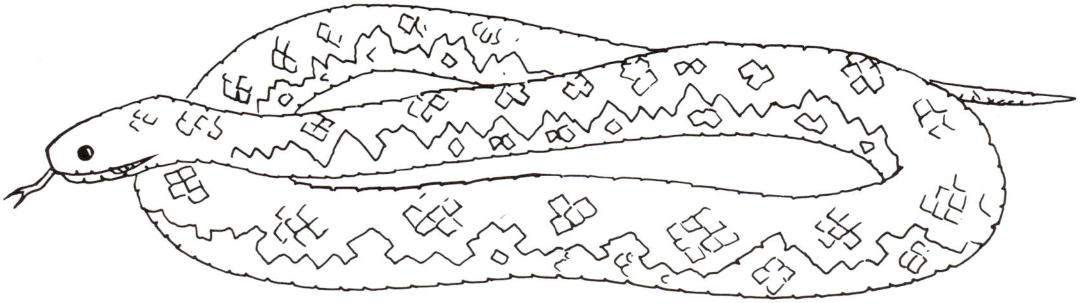

SNAKE SENSE

One animal that suffers from a bad reputation is the snake. Snakes are like any other animal, including humans—they don't like being annoyed. So if you see a snake when you are walking in the bush, observe it carefully, like you would any other animal, but leave it alone.

Diamond pythons, like other snakes, have no external limbs to help them move. Humans use their hands and feet, some birds use their wings, but a snake uses its muscles, its flexible backbone and the dry scales that cover its body. These scales grip the surface on which the snake is moving.

Snakes alive

What you need:
card
white paper
felt-tip pens
scissors
glue
thread

What to do:
Trace the spiral pattern, diagram 4, onto a piece of card. Cut the white paper into round scales. Stick the scales onto the outline. Colour the scales in black, olive and yellow to make a diamond python. Cut out the spiral and use the thread to hang it from the ceiling.

PYTHON WAVE

Now try this

Have your friends stand side by side, holding hands, in a long straight line. The person at the front begins the wave by raising their hand and lifting up their friend's hand which they are holding. The friend then lifts their other hand and the hand of the person next to them. And so on along the line. When the last couple have raised their hands, the leader starts again. This makes a wave pattern—a little like the way a snake moves.

Try this snake activity with some friends.

Lie bellies down on the ground. Clasp your hands behind your backs and keep your feet together. Now try and move. Make sure that you don't try and use your toes to help you.

Hard to move, isn't it?

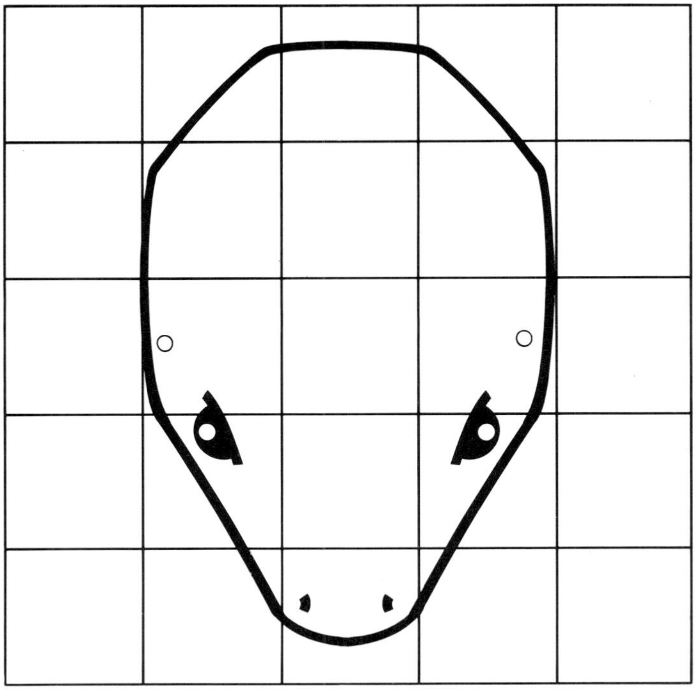

Diamond python mask

Draw a grid on a large piece of card and then copy the outline square by square. Cut around the outline, cut holes for the eyes and mouth and draw in the other features.

EASTERN QUOLL

This small marsupial is sometimes called a native cat—a misleading name because the quoll isn't at all catlike.

Eastern quolls make their dens in disused burrows, hollow logs and even haysheds during the daytime, and prowl the countryside looking for food at night. They eat a wide variety of food including insects, fruits, grasses, and small animals like bandicoots and birds. They are also scavengers and will eat carcasses left behind by other animals.

The female eastern quoll may give birth to as many as thirty young at one time. However only the first six to find one of the six nipples in her pouch will survive. When they are too big for the pouch, the young stay in the den. They are weaned five months after birth. If the female changes dens she carries the young from one den to another on her back.

The eastern quoll is now common only in Tasmania.

SPOT THAT QUOLL

Nocturnal animals like the quoll use camouflage to protect themselves. The spotted coat of the quoll helps it to hide from predators. As the shadows of the bushes fall on its spotted coat, the quoll seems to disappear from sight.

Collect some different coloured toothpicks, a variety of coloured buttons and some ice-block sticks. Count how many items you have, record the number and then scatter them over a small area in your garden, or in the nocturnal bush world you have created. Now with some friends try and find all the objects that you have scattered.

You can also play this game using bits of cardboard, some old cotton reels and some pieces of old wool. Colour the cardboard and the cotton reels to match the natural colours in the garden. Then place these objects in the garden, next to the natural things that are the same colour and see if your friends can find them all.

Eastern quoll mask

Draw a grid on a large piece of card and then copy the outline square by square. Cut around the outline, cut holes for the eyes and mouth and draw in the other features.

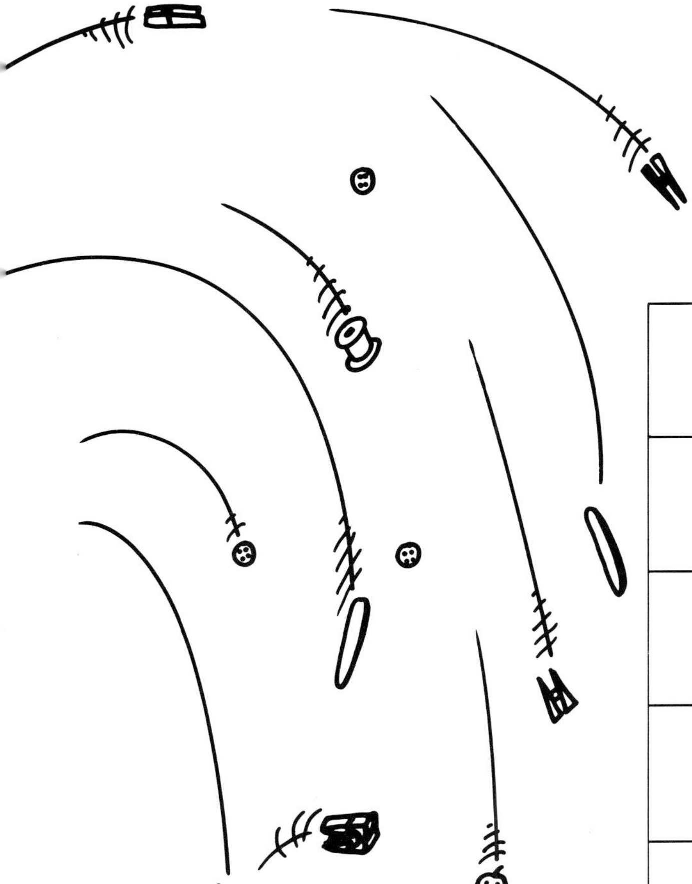

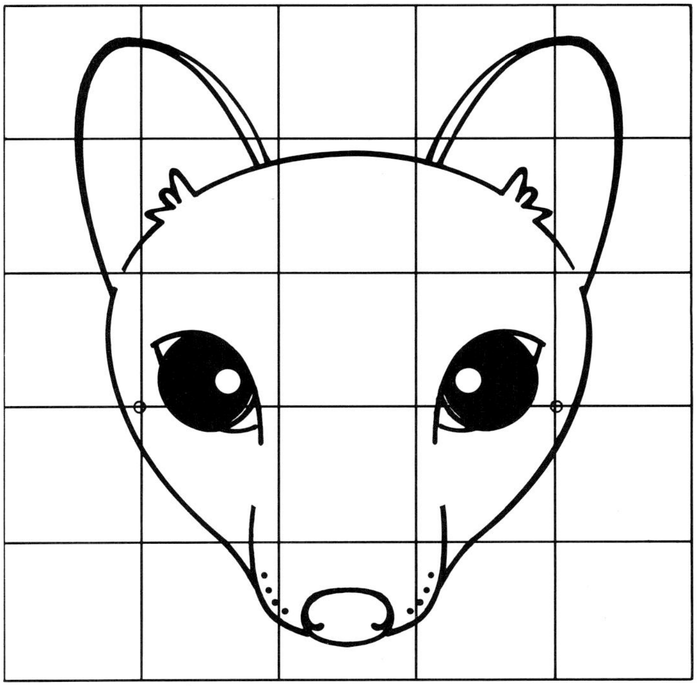

FERAL CAT

The domestic cat was introduced to Australia by the early European settlers. Cats which escaped to the bush very quickly became a direct threat to the native wildlife.

This animal has no natural enemies. Not only does it compete with native animals for food, it feeds on them too. Its diet includes small reptiles, birds and mammals, up to the size of brushtail possums, many of whom are facing extinction.

In the wild this animal will spend much of the day resting in sheltered areas. It comes out at night and roams the bush in search of wildlife.

The female cat will usually have two litters a year with four or five young in each litter.

Unfortunately this animal is found in habitats all over Australia.

CAT CONTROL

Like the feral cat, your pet cat can also cause problems for our native wildlife. There are a few things you can do to enjoy the beauty of our native Australian animals and the friendship of your pet cat.

1 Keep your pet cat locked inside at night. That way the nocturnal native animals can peacefully go about their nocturnal activities.

2 Put a small bell on your cat's collar. When your cat is stalking an animal the bell will scare them off.

3 If your cat has kittens make sure that they go to a good home, or to the RSPCA. Never ever take them and leave them in the bush where they would grow into feral killers of our native animals. Best of all, have your cat desexed.

CAT'S NIGHT OUT

Play this game with some friends. It highlights the danger our native animals face every night.

Who and what you need:
1 cat
possums
4–6 chairs, depending on the number of possums
collars with bells (make collars out of wool, cotton, string)

What to do:
Choose one person as a cat, the rest are possums. Place the chairs around a large area. Have the cat and possums go down on all fours. The object of the game is for the cat to catch the possums as they crawl around the chairs. Once the cat touches a possum that possum becomes a cat and can join in the hunt for possums.

When all the possums have become cats, play the game again but this time put a collar and bell around the cat's neck. As a possum is caught it puts on a collar and bell. Do the bells make it easier for the possums to escape?

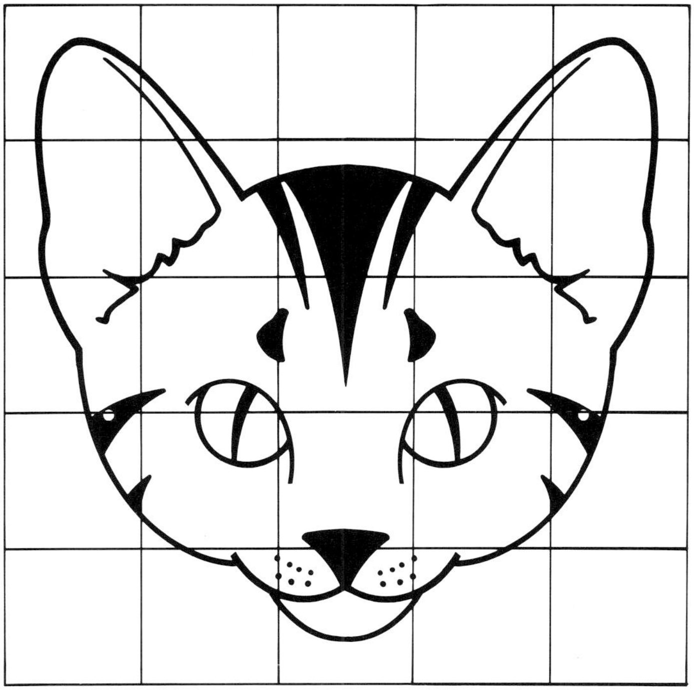

Feral cat mask

Draw a grid on a large piece of card and then copy the outline square by square. Cut around the outline, cut holes for the eyes and mouth and draw in the other features.

GRASS OWL

Owls are very successful nocturnal hunters. Their soft feathers make little noise when they fly. Their eyes, unlike most birds, are in front of their heads making it easy for them to judge distances as they swoop down on their prey. Owls grab hold of their prey with their powerful, sharp talons and use their beaks to rip into the flesh.

The grass owl is the rarest of all Australian owls. It lives in the dense grassy areas of the eastern coast of Queensland. Many owls roost in trees or caves but during the day the grass owl squats in grassy tussocks on the ground. At dusk it silently flies off hunting for rats and mice, which it finds with its keen sight and sharp hearing.

The grass owl usually breeds between March and June, after the heavy rains of the wet season are over. The female grass owl lays between three and eight eggs. The young grass owls are able to fly when they are two months old.

During the daytime grass owls may be seen sunning themselves by spreading their wings and dipping their heads.

NIGHT EYES

No animal can see in total darkness. Owls and some other nocturnal animals have large eyes to catch as much of the night light as possible.

Have an eyeful of your eye

Stand outside while the sun is still out and look at your eyeball in a mirror. Now move into a darkened room, and look again at your eye. What has happened? Try this with a friend. Look at each others' eyes outside in the light and then inside in the shade. Notice how your pupils change size.

At night sit outside and write down all the things you can see. Don't guess, write down exactly what you can see. Do the same thing in daytime. What things did you miss out on?

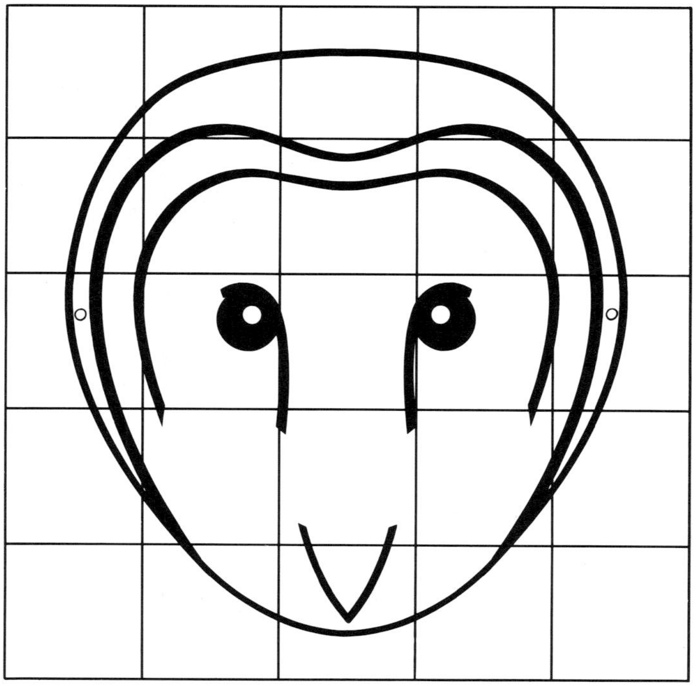

Grass owl mask

Draw a grid on a large piece of card and then copy the outline square by square. Cut around the outline, cut holes for the eyes and mouth and draw in the other features.

Draw the outlines of the animals and plants you saw on stiff pieces of black paper or card. Cut the silhouettes out and use them as decorations.

GREY-HEADED FLYING-FOX

Flying-foxes are members of the bat family—the only mammals capable of true flight. Often at dusk you will see grey-headed flying-foxes travelling across the sky. They are moving from their daytime resting camps to night-time feeding camps. Their favourite foods are nectar, blossoms and native fruits.

Occasionally flying-foxes will raid fruit orchards, but only if they can't find native fruits to eat. The flying-fox pulps the fruit it is eating in its mouth, takes in all the juices and then spits out the fibres. It doesn't swallow the fibres because they would make it too heavy to fly.

The flying-fox wraps its wing around itself for protection from rain and to keep warm. Each wing has a thumb claw which is used for grooming and also to hang by.

No bats are blind. Flying-foxes have very large eyes which together with a good sense of smell help them find food.

Flying-foxes, like all bats, are placental mammals which means that when the young are born they have all their body features, they just need to grow. At birth, generally between October and early November, they cling to their mother with their feet while their teeth are attached to a nipple. They are covered with fine fur.

MAKE YOUR OWN GREY-HEADED FLYING-FOX

People often say that bats' wings look very much like umbrellas, and if you look closely at their wings you may think that this is so. The bat's wings are covered with a thin membrane, like the covering of an umbrella, and the wing bones are like the rib cage of an umbrella.

What you need:
two sheets of black cardboard
glue
string
scissors
pin
grey, red, brown felt-tip pens

What to do:
Cut out two rectangles. Trace the shape below and then cut it out. Fold along the lines, as shown. Glue the wing sections of the two bat halves together, leaving the middle section open as the bat's body. Colour the bat's head grey and its neck a red-brown colour. Use the

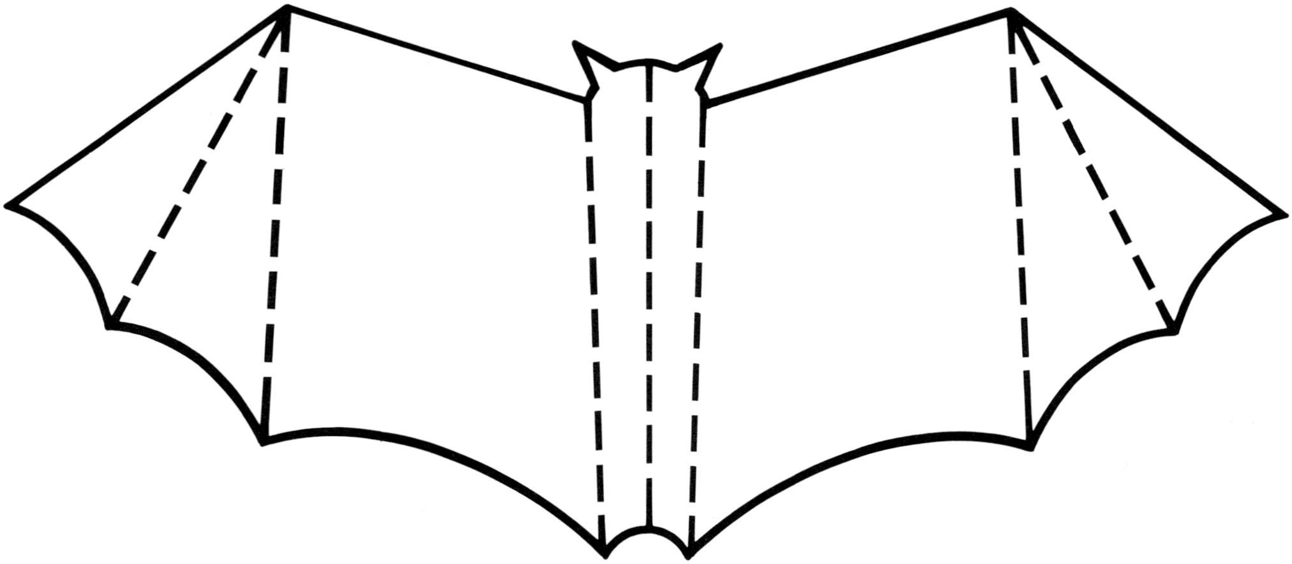

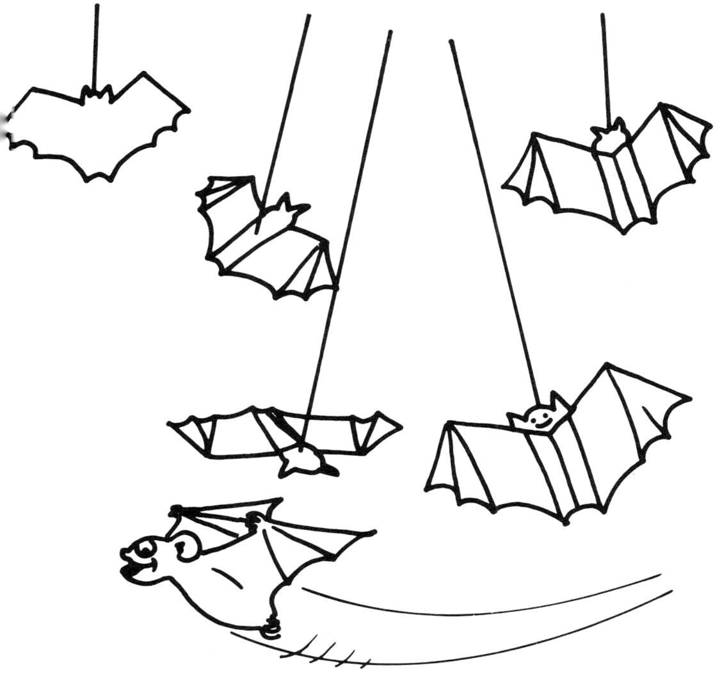

pin to make two small holes in the top half of the bat's body and thread through the cotton or string. Use the bat as a decoration for your party, or hang it above your bed and have a batty bedroom.

Grey-headed flying-fox mask

Draw a grid on a large piece of card and then copy the outline square by square. Cut around the outline, cut holes for the eyes and mouth and draw in the other features.

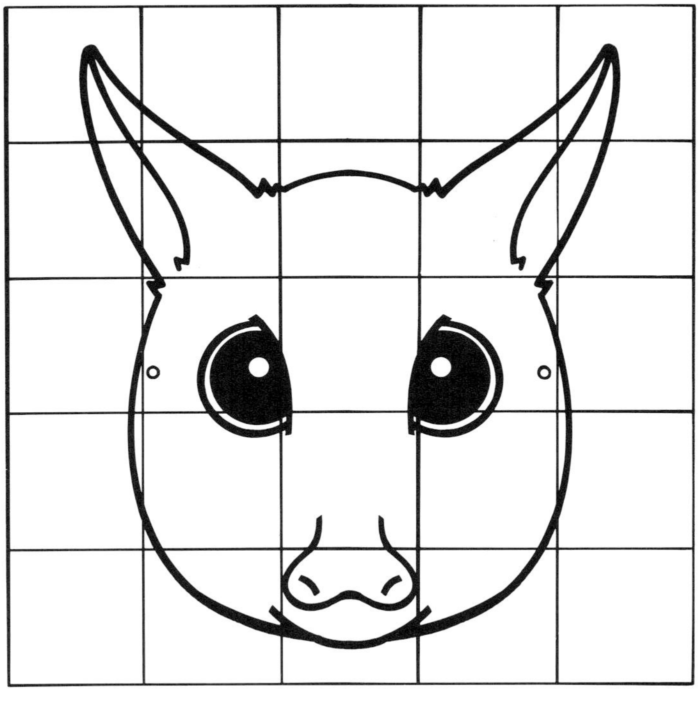

LEADBEATER'S POSSUM

This small possum, thought to be extinct until 1961, lives in colonies of up to eight individuals. These possums build communal nests of shredded bark in hollows in mountain ash trees in the Victorian highlands.

The Leadbeater's possum is a rapid mover, especially if it is disturbed, it leaps from tree to tree and runs along the branches, gripping with its sharp claws as it goes.

Insects which feed on the leaves and under the bark of the mountain ash, nectar, and gum from certain wattle trees are this possum's main foods.

The young are usually born in May and June or October and November. They stay in the female's pouch attached to one of the four nipples. There are usually only two possums in a litter.

This marsupial is very rare and habitat destruction through forest clearing and repeated bushfires could mean extinction.

POSSUM POMANDER

Make a sweet smelling ball to hang around your burrow.

What you need:
1 orange
2 packets of cloves
ground cinnamon
string
a button

What to do:
Tie a button to one end of a piece of string. Ask an adult to thread a darning needle with the string and then push it through the orange. Cover your orange with cloves by pushing the pointed ends of the cloves through the orange peel. Place the orange in a bag, add a tablespoon of cinnamon, close the bag and give it a good shake. Take the orange out of the bag, blow off the extra cinnamon dust and hang up your orange smelling ball.

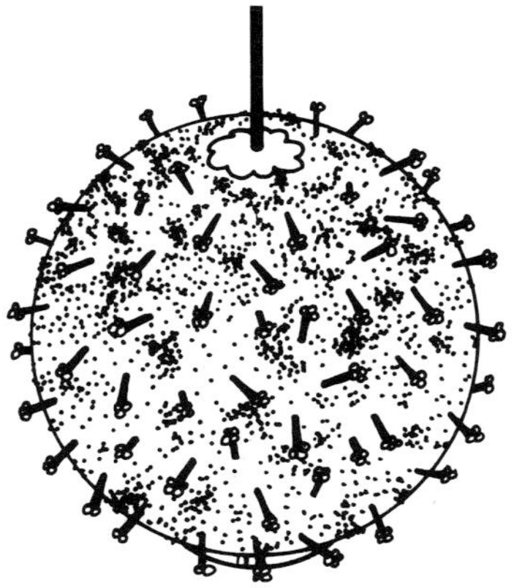

Leadbeater's possum mask

Draw a grid on a large piece of card and then copy the outline square by square. Cut around the outline, cut holes for the eyes and mouth and draw in the other features.

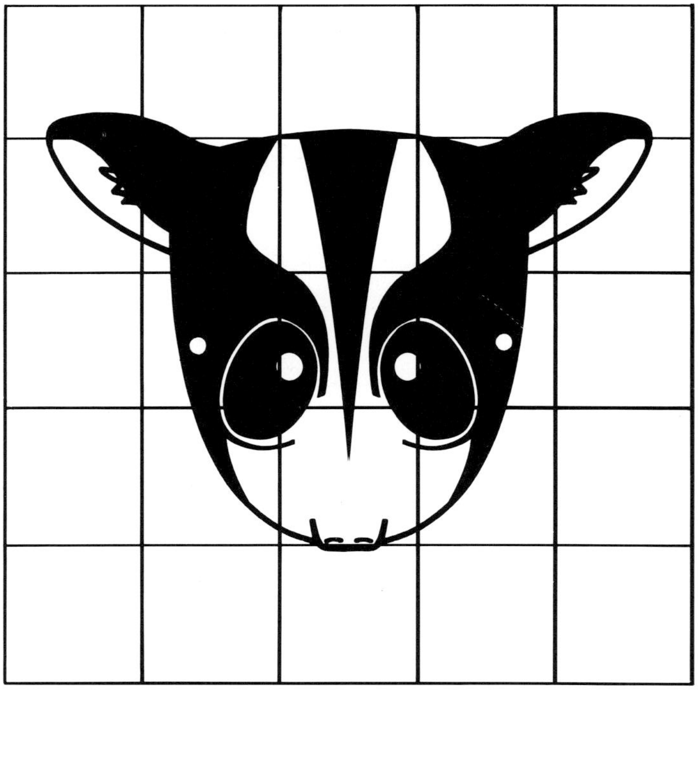

FRUIT SMOOTHIES

What you need:
fruit
cup
blender
crushed ice

What to do:
Peel and chop ½ cup ripe fruit, place in blender with ½ cup of your favourite fruit juice. Add ¼ cup of crushed ice and blend again.

Try one of these delicious combinations: bananas, passionfruit and orange juice; strawberries and pineapple juice; pineapple, apples and orange juice; apples, pears and apricot juice.

LESSER LONG-EARED BAT

Flying-foxes roost in the open, but the smaller insectivorous bats, some of them smaller than your hand, sleep in caves, tree hollows, or even under house eaves. These bats use echolocation to find their food. As the bat flies, it sends out high pitched sounds which hit objects in their pathway. This may be a tree—an obstacle to fly around—or an insect—food to eat. The sound bounces back off the object and is picked up by the bat's very sensitive ears.

These bats fold their wings against the sides of their bodies when they are roosting, unlike flying-foxes which wrap their wings around themselves.

The young bats are born hairless and suckle on a nipple in their mother's armpit. When the female bat goes hunting for food, she leaves her young behind in a nursery cave which may have more than one hundred other bats.

The lesser long-eared bat is found over most of Australia, except north-eastern Queensland.

This bat has adapted very well to living near humans, even to roosting in clothing left on washing lines. When hunting for food this bat flies very near to the ground, and as a result is a food source for domestic cats.

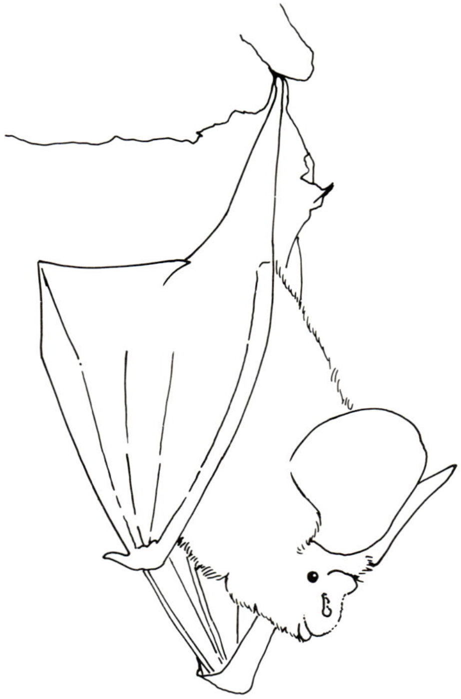

EAR I AM

Insectivorous bats rely on echo-location to guide them.

Gather some friends together in a clear playing area. Choose someone to be the 'bat' and then blindfold them. Divide the rest of your friends into two groups. One group become objects, for example a tree, rock, cliff, branch, and one group become food, for example a fly, mosquito, beetle and so on. The 'bat' has to walk/fly across the playing area listening to the objects and the food calling their names—'tree', 'rock', 'insect' and so on. The 'bat' must not touch the objects but has to catch the food. Once a 'food' is caught, it becomes the 'bat' and so the game goes on.

SPIDER DELIGHT

What you need:
lemonade
ice-cream
hundreds and thousands
dessertspoon
ice-cream scoop

What to do:
Place a spoonful of ice-cream in a large cup. Pour the lemonade halfway up the cup. Add a scoop of ice-cream and then top up with more lemonade. Sprinkle hundreds and thousands on top.

Mmm, delicious!

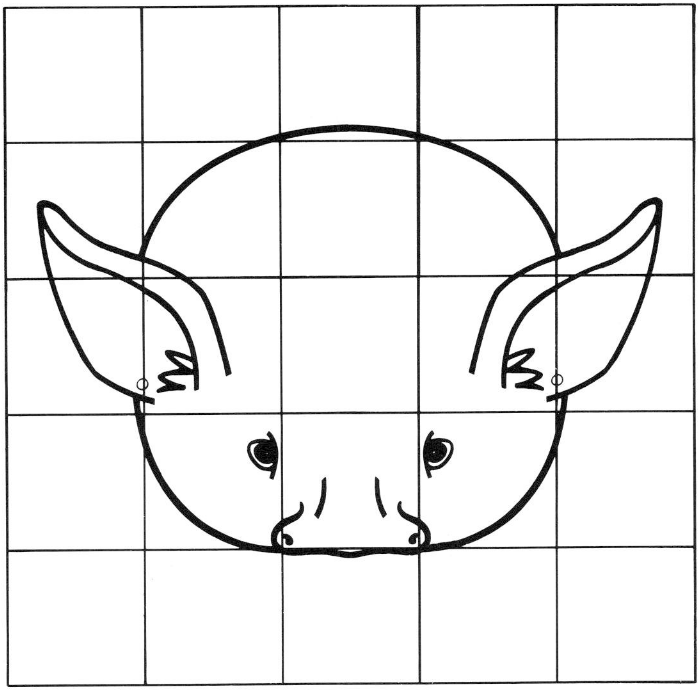

Insectivorous bat mask

Draw a grid on a large piece of card and then copy the outline square by square. Cut around the outline, cut holes for the eyes and mouth and draw in the other features.

MITCHELL'S HOPPING MOUSE

As it hops around on its very long hind legs this mouse looks just like a mini kangaroo. Its tail has a little tuft of fluff on the end and is longer than the combined length of its head and body.

During the daytime the hopping mouse shelters in deep burrows, which it digs with its paws. Up to four hopping mice will live together in a system of burrows. At night-time the hopping mouse comes out of its burrow and goes searching for seeds, leaves and the small insects on which it feeds. Its long sharp teeth grow throughout its life.

The female usually gives birth to three or four young in a litter. They are weaned when they are five weeks old.

Mitchell's hopping mouse is found in sandy woody areas of southern Australia.

HIST, HARK

Stop and listen. What sounds can you hear? If you are inside the house you may be able to hear a television set, someone talking, the radio. If you are outside you may be able to hear a car go by, birds twittering, dogs barking, neighbours talking.

Write down all the sounds you can hear. Do the same thing at different times of the day. Record on a cassette the sounds you hear at night-time, in the morning, in your house, under a tree. You can play them as background 'music' at your nocturnal party.

Most of the sounds we hear travel through the air. Go for a swim in a swimming pool and listen to the sounds there. Are the sounds different in the water from the air? Ask a friend to throw a large ball into the pool while you are underwater. Do the same when you are above water. Does the noise change?

Put a watch on a table or on the top of a post. Press your ear against the other end of the table (or the post) and listen to the sounds. Try listening to the sounds through other things—put one ear on the ground, or put a box against one ear.

SOUND MAP

Make a sound map. Every time that you hear a sound record a mark on the paper, and a symbol for that sound just like this:

Try this again one week later. Were there any different sounds? See if a friend can locate the sounds on your sound map.

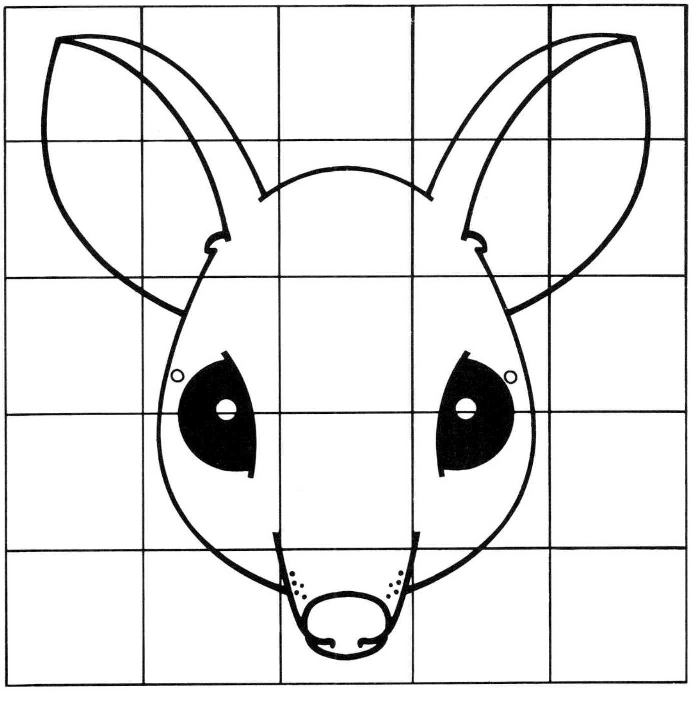

Mitchell's hopping mouse mask

Draw a grid on a large piece of card and then copy the outline square by square. Cut around the outline, cut holes for the eyes and mouth and draw in the other features.

RINGTAIL POSSUM

Like the brushtail possum, ringtails have also adapted well to life with humans, but they aren't as frequent house visitors. Ringtail possums are much smaller than brushtails, and have a very long thin white-tipped tail. The top of the tail is covered in fur but underneath the end is naked so it can grip on tightly when the possum is moving through trees or carrying nesting material. When it is not gripping onto something, the tail is often tightly coiled—just like a spring.

Ringtails collect leaves, twigs and small branches and then form these into hollow balls to make their nests. This nest, called a drey, is often well hidden. At other times the ringtail will line a tree hollow with nesting material to make its drey.

Ringtails eat mainly leaves but they add to this diet with fruits and blossoms. Ringtails who nest near humans often steal and eat rose petals.

Young ringtail possums spend four months in the female's pouch attached to one of four teats. There are usually only two offspring in the pouch. After they leave the pouch, the young possums spend the next two months suckling in the drey and riding on the female's back while she forages for food.

Ringtail possums live in the forested areas along the east coast of Australia.

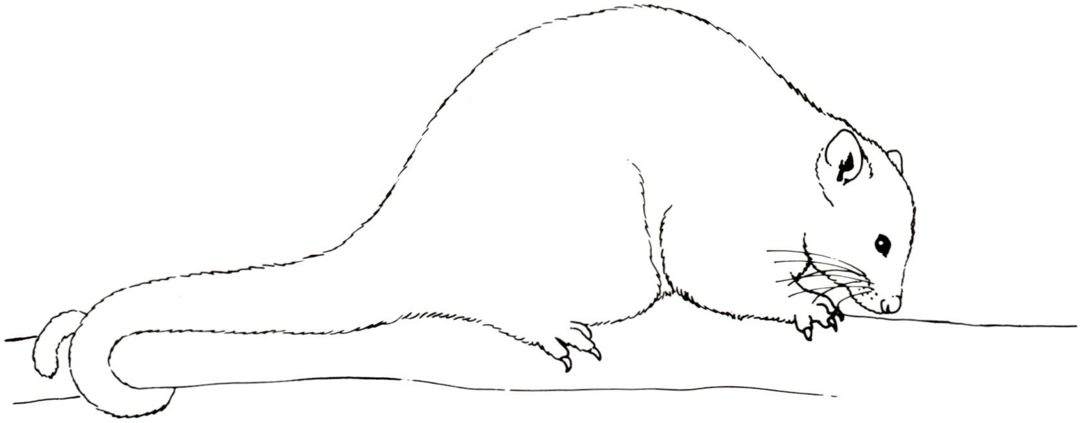

POSSUM PRYING

When the sun has set and the nocturnal animals are starting to come out, go and sit outside in the garden or ask an adult to take you to a nature reserve or, if you're lucky, out into the bush. Let your eyes adjust to the light and then watch the trees for possums. Plot on paper the paths the possums take through the trees. Don't forget to mark on the paper where you are. Record the possum movements over a few nights. Use different coloured pencils. Do they use the same trees? Same branches? Do they follow the same paths?

Remember to keep quiet—too much noise and you won't see any nocturnal creatures. If you are watching at home, you may want to make a possum-watching notice to warn your family to keep quiet too.

POSSUM SALAD

Cut up and mix together pieces of apples, pears, bananas, watermelon, strawberries, pawpaw, pineapple, mango and grapes. Squeeze an orange and pour the juice over your salad.

Possums eat blossoms from native plants as well, so include some chopped up mint leaves in your fruit salad.

Ringtail possum mask

Draw a grid on a large piece of card and then copy the outline square by square. Cut around the outline, cut holes for the eyes and mouth and draw in the other features.

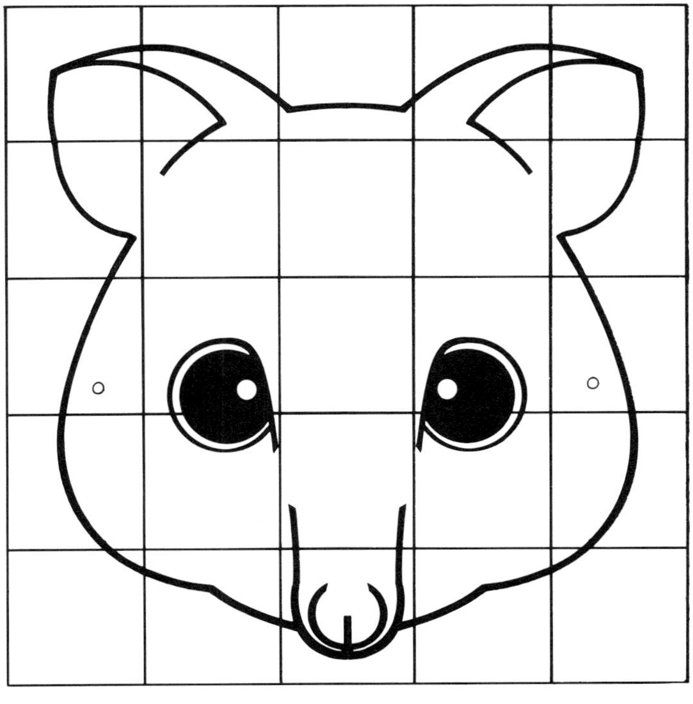

SPOTTED CUSCUS

With its flat face, thick fur, small ears, and eyes at the front of its head, the spotted cuscus could be mistaken for a monkey as it climbs slowly and deliberately through the trees. Like the ringtail possum, the spotted cuscus's tail is prehensile—it will wind around a branch and grasp it firmly.

The spotted cuscus sleeps in the trees through the day, sometimes even pulling branches around itself to hide behind. At night it forages for flowers, leaves, and fruits. Occasionally it will catch and eat small birds and mammals.

Although the female spotted cuscus has four teats in her pouch she usually rears only one young. The young spotted cuscus rides on its mother's back until it is old enough to be on its own.

Spotted cuscuses can be found in the rainforest areas of the Cape York Peninsula.

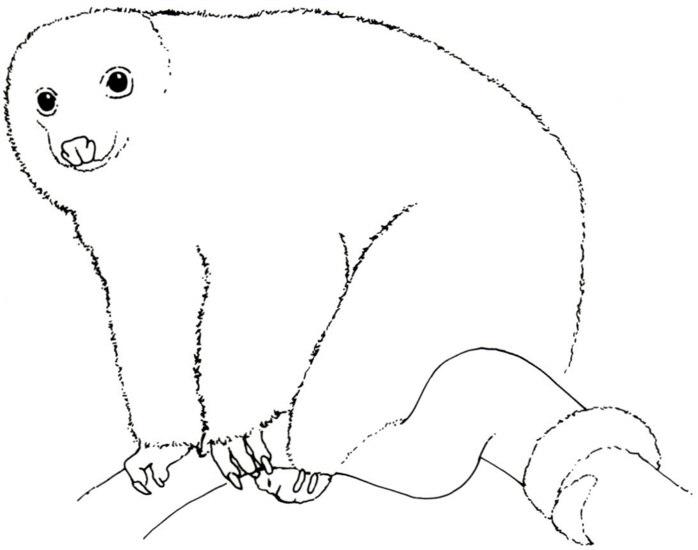

CUSCUS CRAWL

With its toes and its scaly tail tightly gripped around a branch, the cuscus is nearly immovable.

Play this slow and silent movement game with your friends. The object of the game is for players to try and move around a set area as slowly as possible. Ask everyone to go down on the floor in a crawling position. Play some really slow music and watch carefully as everyone moves in slow motion. Anyone who stops is out of the game.

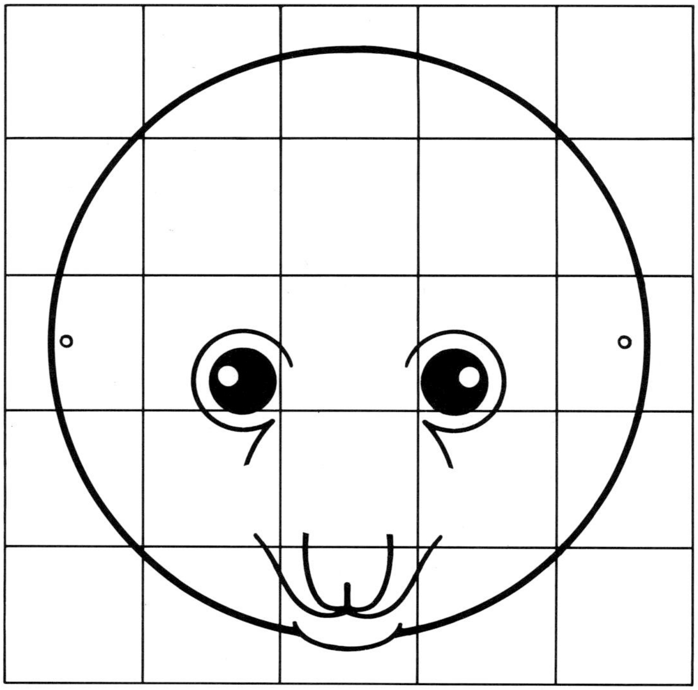

Cuscus mask

Draw a grid on a large piece of card and then copy the outline square by square. Cut around the outline, cut holes for the eyes and mouth and draw in the other features.

CUSCUS MOBILE

What you need:
white card
scissors
felt-tip pen
black thread
4 pieces of dowelling 25 cm long
a pin

What to do:
Trace six cuscus outlines onto the card. Cut out the outlines and draw in eyes, nose and ears, as shown. Use the pin to push a hole through the middle of the cuscuses' backs, as marked. Assemble as shown.

TASMANIAN DEVIL

The Tasmanian devil, the largest of the Australian carnivorous marsupials, isn't as fierce as its name or its looks imply. It roams at night in search of its food and spends the daytime resting in hollow logs or caves.

Tasmanian devils will eat meat of any kind even from mammals bigger than themselves, but they prefer to eat carrion—meat already dead. With their sharp teeth and powerful jaws they are able to eat any part of a dead animal—even its skull, bones and all.

The female Tasmanian devil has a backwardly opening pouch that carries up to four young attached to the nipples. The young leave the pouch when they are 15 weeks old but stay in the nest while their mother is feeding.

Tasmanian devils are common in Tasmania, where they can be found living not only in the forests but also in the outer suburbs of country towns.

WHISKERS AND BRISTLES

Some nocturnal animals, like the Tasmanian devil, have very sensitive bristles or whiskers on the sides of their faces. These help them find their way around at night-time.

These bristles are just like your fingertips. Imagine having fingertips on the side of your face. Watch a cat move around a room and notice how its whiskers touch the walls. Seals use their bristles to detect movement in the water.

Use your fingertips to see. Sit on the ground and close your eyes. Feel the ground and all the things around you. Have a friend join you. Blindfold your friend and then give them things to feel. Ask them to tell you what they are feeling. Swap over and ask your friend to give you things to feel. Walk along feeling the walls of your house—either inside or outside—with your fingertips. It's an interesting way of finding your way around!

DEVILBURGERS

What you need:
500 grams minced chicken or lamb
4 hamburger buns, split and toasted on one side
8 slices of cheese (optional)
butter or margarine
paprika
salt and pepper
friendly, helpful adult
knife to spread with

What to do:
1 Ask an adult to heat the griller for you.
2 Divide meat into eight equal pieces.
3 Spread untoasted sides of the buns with butter or margarine and then with a thin layer of meat.
4 Season with salt and pepper.
5 Ask an adult to place the buns under the griller and grill for five minutes.
6 If using cheese, place on top of the meat and grill for one extra minute.
7 Sprinkle with paprika.
8 Serve whole or cut into strips for finger food.

Tasmanian devil mask

Draw a grid on a large piece of card and then copy the outline square by square. Cut around the outline, cut holes for the eyes and mouth and draw in the other features.

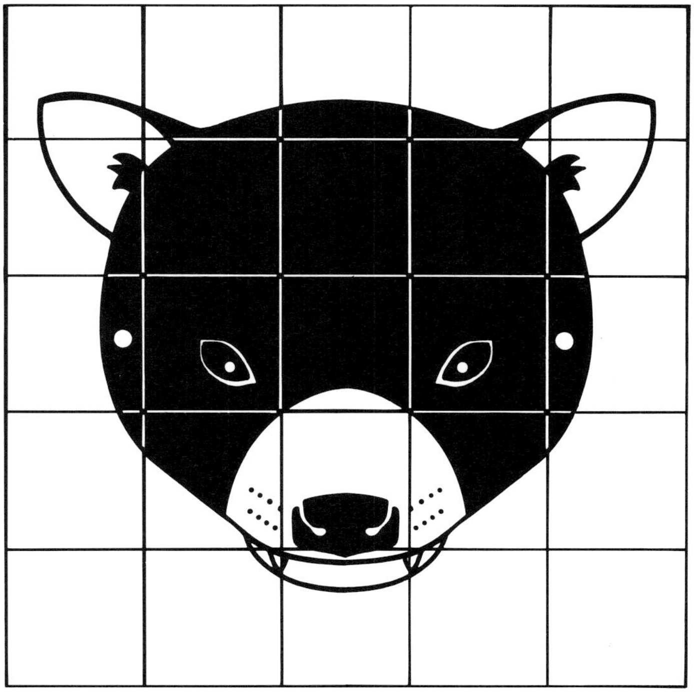

Cheng, Christopher.

Eyespy book of night creatures.

ISBN 0 86896 590 1.

1. Nocturnal animals—Australia—Juvenile literature.
I. Title.

591.994

Illustrations for animal masks and activities by Michael Davis.
Cover photograph of grey-headed flying-fox and back cover photograph by Ken Dolling.

Photograph of bilby by Reg Morrison/Auscape International.
Photographs of brush-tailed phascogale and Mitchell's hopping mouse by Hans and Judy Beste/Auscape International.
Photographs of brushtail possum, common wombat, diamond python, ringtail possum, Tasmanian devil, and Leadbeater's possum by Jean Paul Ferrero/Auscape International.
Photographs of spotted cuscus, juvenile grass owls, lesser long-eared bat courtesy of Taronga Zoo.
Photograph of eastern quoll by D Parer and E Parer-Cook/Auscape International.
Photograph of feral cat by M Gillam/Auscape International.
Photograph of grey-headed flying-fox by Kathie Atkinson/Auscape International.

First published in 1990 by Ashton Scholastic Pty Limited (Inc. in NSW), PO Box 579, Gosford 2250. Also in Brisbane, Melbourne, Adelaide, Perth and Auckland, NZ.

Typeset by David Lake, Forresters Beach NSW.
Text set in 13/15 New Baskerville.
Printed by Griffin Press Limited, Netley SA.
10 9 8 7 6 5 4 3 2 1 0 1 2 3 4 5 / 9